Beginning

GOLF

Bruce Curtis & Jay Morelli

Sterling Publishing Co., Inc.
New York

To Margaret and John Morelli

ACKNOWLEDGMENTS

I would like to thank Bruce Curtis. His talent and sense of humor made this book a lot of fun. Thanks also to Laurie Newton and Bob and Christina Affelder for helping me with the text. Thanks to Cliff Bouchard and all the staff at The Plantation Inn.

I would also like to thank the following models for their help: Elizabeth Walling, Lion Domingo, Dylan Griffin, Ben Story, and Jed Tarr. Special thanks to my friend Ernie Lanford, the golf coach at Florida State University, and the Florida State Golf Team. Thanks to all the staff at The Original Golf School, where I developed my teaching ideas. The most important thank you is to the students at The Original Golf School for supporting our program.

DESIGNED BY WANDA KOSSAK
PHOTOGRAPHY BY BRUCE CURTIS

Library of Congress Cataloging-in-Publication Data Available

10 9 8 7 6 5 4 3 2 1

First paperpack edition published 2001 by
Sterling Publishing Company, Inc.
387 Park Avenue South, New York, N.Y. 10016
© 2000 by Bruce Curtis and Jay Morelli
Distributed in Canada by Sterling Publishing
c/o Canadian Manda Group, One Atlantic Avenue, Suite 105
Toronto, Ontario, Canada M6K 3E7
Distributed in Great Britain and Europe by Chris Lloyd at Orca Book
Services, Stanley House, Fleets Lane, Poole BH15 3AJ, England.
Distributed in Australia by Capricorn Link (Australia) Pty. Ltd.
P.O. Box 704, Windsor, NSW 2756 Australia
Printed in Hong Kong
All rights reserved

Sterling ISBN 0-8069-4970-8 Trade
            0-8069-9081-3 Paper

CONTENTS

INTRODUCTION

It has been a pleasure to have golf instruction as my career. Nothing makes me happier than to see a golfer improve. I've taught PGA and LPGA tour stars as well as people who have never played and I can honestly say that the same smile shines at all levels when the perfect shot is played.

Golf is an amazing game in that it is the mastery of simple fundamentals that produces improvement. The greatest players concentrate on how they hold the club, how they aim at their target, how they stand to the ball, and how they remain in balance. Very often I have taught PGA tour players one day and new players the next, and I have worked on exactly the same fundamentals.

Golf is a wonderfully social game. We all know what it's like to be humbled by a bad shot as we have all known the joy of a solid hit. Golfers share that. Through these experiences we develop friendships and fun that last a lifetime. The best times of my life have been days with my father, John, and my son, Michael, on the course.

This book has basic information for those who are just starting as well as some advanced tips for those who have played for a long time.

I've tried to present fundamental instruction in a building-block approach. The first step is to have good equipment that "fits." I then move to the golf grip, posture and address, a pre-shot routine, and finally the swing motion. I also think you'll enjoy the short-game presentation. The concepts are basic; you just add practice.

This book is also a guide for parents who want to teach their children to play golf or plan to enroll them in golf lessons.

The new wave of great players, led by David Duval, Annika Sorenstam, Karrie Webb, and Tiger Woods, has certainly stirred new interest in this great game. I encourage everyone to take up this game and share the enjoyment.

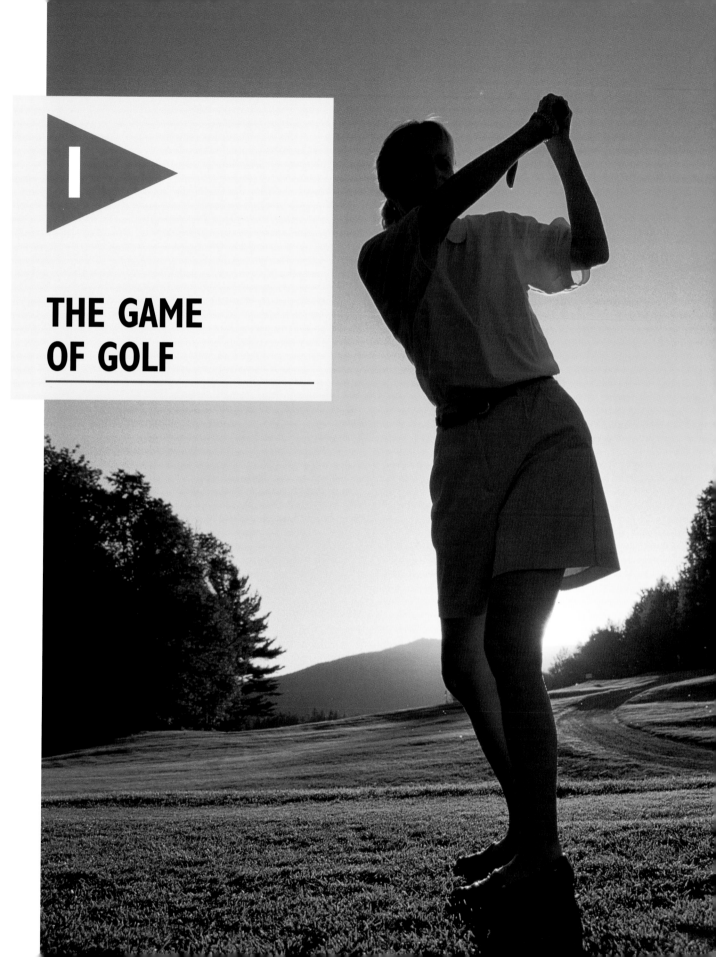

I

THE GAME
OF GOLF

Many with less power easily score better than their longer-hitting competitors. Playing conditions on the course are also constantly changing. How a player adjusts to varying winds, weather, grass, and temperatures are integral steps in becoming a better player. And, of course, how we deal with our own emotions while playing has a great deal to do with our outcome and score. The players who can remain "cool" through the normal course of the round will best recover from problem situations and maximize opportunities during a golf round.

Golf is a wonderful game that we all can enjoy and that no one has ever completely mastered. Go play and enjoy!

The object of the game of golf is to play the course in the fewest possible strokes and, of course, to have fun in the process.

The charm of the game is that since it requires so many varied skills, it gives everyone an opportunity to demonstrate particular strengths. Power is required to deliver long shots, but that power must be tempered with control. Finesse and feel are essential to playing delicate shots around the green.

Oh, the joys of the game!

2

EQUIPMENT

A putter and a ball

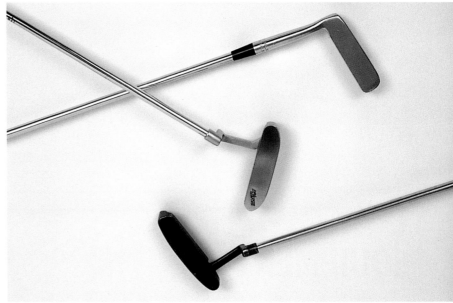

An assortment of different style putters

The game of golf is about 500 years old. Since that time the equipment has progressed from wooden sticks and rocks to highly sophisticated instruments. Many of the materials used in today's equipment, such as titanium, were developed through the NASA space programs. The same materials with properties to develop lighter and faster spacecraft are also used to make golf clubs lighter and easier to play.

A set of golf clubs. The rules of golf allow a player to carry 14 golf clubs. While there is no set requirement as to how many woods or irons a player carries, there are some general guidelines.

1. *Putter.* The one club every golfer carries is the putter. The putter is the shortest club in the bag and is used on the green. It is sometimes used for short shots just off the green.

2. *Metal Woods.* Woods, commonly referred to as "metal woods" (originally they were made of wood but now are made of a variety of different metals), are the clubs used to

achieve the most distance. They are numbered 1 to 7 depending on length of the club and the loft or "pitch" of the club face.

The #1 wood, or driver, is the longest club a player uses and has the least loft and therefore produces the most distance. The driver is used off the tee when a player is starting to play most par 4 and par 5 holes. The fairway woods are used when a player has a long distance to the green. (As the number on the club increases, the length it is designed to hit the golf ball decreases. Therefore, a 3 wood is designed to hit a longer shot than a 5 wood. Most golfers use #1, 3, and 5 woods in their set.)

An assortment of woods and metal woods

A typical metal wood driver

3. *Irons.* The irons are accuracy clubs. Like the metal woods, they are numbered by length. The lowest numbered iron is generally the 3 iron, with a set normally going to the 9 iron. The 3 iron will produce the most distance of these accuracy clubs, while the 9 iron produces the highest and shortest results. There are also two irons called "wedges" that are designed to hit short shots around the greens. The pitching wedge is designed for high, soft shots around the green, while the sand wedge is designed for play in the sand out of greenside bunkers. The wedges are the shortest irons and have the most loft.

A set of clubs

Golf shoes and clubs

At the driving range the player should hit every club and determine how far he or she hits the ball with each club. This is the first step to "managing" your way around the course.

4. *Footwear.* Golf shoes are specifically designed to provide support as well as traction. The most popular golf shoe now has "soft spikes," rubber or plastic spikes that provide traction. Originally these spikes were made of steel. While proper golf shoes are preferred because of their support, you can also play in comfortable rubber-soled shoes.

5. *Golf glove.* Many players prefer to play with a golf glove on their left hand (left-handed golfers play with a glove on their right hand). While this is not essential, it does provide extra grip as you hold onto the club.

Golf balls and tees

Sets of clubs on a bag rack

A golf ball teed up at the proper height

What type of clubs should I buy? The most important feature in buying a set of clubs is that they "fit" the player. Manufacturers develop clubs that are based on the norm, but in many cases a player needs some adjustments from that norm to have the clubs properly fit. While the rules of golf allow for 14 clubs, new players may start with a simple "starter set" that includes about 10 clubs. Starter sets vary, but might typically include a 3, 5, and 7 metal wood; a 5, 7, and 9 iron; a pitching wedge; a sand wedge; and a putter.

Hand-me-down sets are usually not a good idea as there have been many improvements in club design as well as materials. These improvements make it much easier for beginners to learn the game.

New and experienced players alike should play with metal woods and perimeter-weighted irons. Perimeter-weighted or cavity-back irons expand the "sweet spot" on the club face and are more forgiving for balls not hit dead center.

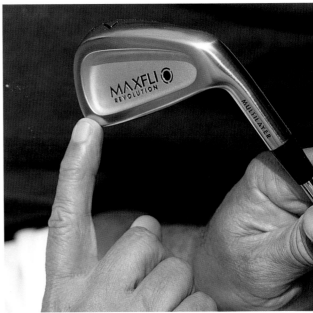

Illustrating a perimeter-weighted design

Following are the basic considerations for club-fitting:

1. *Grip size.* The width of the handle of the club will vary, but the player should be able to wrap his or her fingers around the handle easily. If the handle is too thick, the natural wrist action will not occur during the swing.

2. *Shaft flex.* The shaft of the golf club is a spring. It will actually bend from the power generated by a swing. The amount that it bends can be determined and that amount should maximize power without giving up control.

3. *Length.* The correct length of the club is determined by the player's height, arm length, and swing characteristics. A tall player with long arms would probably play with a fairly standard length golf club. There is no exact formula for determining club length. "Fitting" a player for a set of clubs is best done by a club-fitting specialist. While high-quality clubs will ensure a consistent club, they will not necessarily be best for the player. The most important feature is that the clubs fit the individual.

4. *Lie.* The club head for each club must sit properly on the ground, as this affects accuracy. Once again, the correct lie should be determined by a club-fitting specialist.

3

THE FULL
SWING

As with every sport, golf has certain fundamentals. These fundamentals are designed to promote power as well as control. They are designed to create a smooth, balanced, rhythmical golf swing.

1. *The golf grip* is simply how you hold the handle of the golf club. It will establish the pattern and look of your swing. Begin by holding the club waist-high so that the leading edge of the club face is square to the target. You will achieve this if the leading edge is perpendicular to the ground. Now hold the club first in your left hand (left-handed players reverse) so that you control the club with the fingers of your left hand. You will notice a "V" formed by your thumb and index finger that should point to your right shoulder. The handle of the club should be underneath the pad of the left hand so the wrists can hinge properly on the backswing. Now place your right hand on the club so that you hold the club in the fingers. The "V" formed by your right thumb and forefinger should also point to your right shoulder. To join the hands so they work together, interlock the right pinkie with your left index

To develop the proper grip, begin with the club waist high.

Tilt from the hips to get into a good posture.

In the proper golf grip, the handle of the club is supported by the left forefinger and the pad of the left hand. This will ensure the proper hinging or wrist action during the swing.

Widen your stance to establish balance.

finger, overlap (also called the Vardon grip), or simply keep a 10-finger grip.

You should have no tension when you hold the golf club. Tension will reduce power and control by inhibiting the free swinging motion of the golf club. Grip pressure is best described as medium to light. You should hold the club softly enough to feel the weight of the head of the club.

The golf grip will have a big influence on your golf swing. If the grip is correct you will find it easy to attain the proper address position and then cre-

ate a smooth and rhythmical golf swing.

2. *Posture* can mean different things to different people. To a soldier it might mean standing straight and tall. In golf it means something quite different.

Posture in golf is simply a good athletic starting position from which to make the golf swing. To develop the correct golf grip, hold the club waist-high, with the upper arms lightly touching your chest. Now simply tilt from the hips to allow the club head to reach the ground.

An inverted V formed by the left thumb and left forefinger should point to the right shoulder.

When you place the right hand on the club, the V formed by the right thumb and right forefinger should also point to the right shoulder.

The distance you stand from the ball is a result of the tilt and the length of the club. The wedge is the shortest club you swing. As you progress to longer clubs you will stand farther from the ball.

To achieve a balanced stance, the player should push the hips back a little so that some weight is on the heels. This action counterbalances the effect of tilting from the hips. In a balanced address position you should be able to wiggle your toes. If you can't, you're leaning forward too much. You should be in a balanced position front to back and side to side. This position should be comfortable. It is similar to the "athletic position" referred to in many other sports, such as the position of the fielder in baseball or a basketball player awaiting a pass.

3. *The address position.* At the address position you should have a good grip and posture. The ball should be approximately in the middle of your stance for the shorter clubs and more forward in your stance for longer clubs until it is inside the heel of your front foot with a driver. A line across your feet should be approximately parallel to the intended line of flight.

Good posture is a well-balanced starting position.

This is called a "square stance." For some specialty shots, use an "open" stance. In this stance a line across the toes, shoulders, and hips points to the left of the target. This stance is often used to play short shots, particularly out of sand bunkers. For other specialty shots, use a "closed" stance. In this stance a line across the toes, shoulders, and hips points to the right of the target.

Your feet should be as wide apart as is necessary for balance on each shot. For long shots your feet should be about as wide apart as your shoulders. Your stance becomes more narrow on shorter shots.

The right foot should be square to the line of flight while the left foot should be flared out slightly to promote an easy turn toward the target and follow through.

Good posture is illustrated here: it should have some flex at the knees and tilting from the waist. Notice that the player is totally in balance.

4. *The Pre-Shot Routine.* Many golfers easily hit shot after shot in the practice area only to find that when they go to the course, they do not hit the shots nearly as well. In the practice area, we swing freely. On the course, often we feel tension and do not experience the same feeling of ease. There is a way to carry over the feeling of ease from the practice tee to the golf course.

This system is called a "pre-shot routine."

All the best players have a consistent routine. A good pre-shot routine will set up the player to repeat sound fundamentals even in tournament or pressure situations.

The first step is to plan the shot. If you are playing a tee shot, you want to determine the ideal spot to aim for. On an

approach shot you must determine the yardage to the green, if you are uphill or downhill, the speed and direction of the wind, and how much the ball will roll. Expert players will also try to aim at the pin or a certain section of the green. On short shots close to the green you still should plan your shot. All of these considerations are made before you even choose which club you will use for the shot. Once you have created a clear plan, proceed with the pre-shot routine.

We all have our own pace. Some people walk and talk faster than others. The pre-shot routine should reflect that. A "fast mover" might assess the shot, address the ball, look at the target once, and swing, all in a few seconds. A slower player might assess the shot, take 10 seconds to address the ball, look at the target four or five times, and then swing.

While every player will establish his or her own steps and pace, make sure your routine includes the following:

A. Establish the line of flight by standing behind the ball and drawing an imaginary line from the ball to the target.

The triangle (formed by an imaginary line across the shoulders and arms) and the club move together...

The weight of the body moves toward the right foot to support the swinging action of the club...

Notice how the wrists are beginning to "hinge"; this is not a conscious move but the result of the proper golf grip.

B. As you start to address the ball take your grip, square the club head, set your back foot square to the line, then set your front foot. Once comfortable, look at your target once or twice and then swing away. The entire routine should be done smoothly and take only four to seven seconds.

As you address the ball and go through your pre-shot routine, it is essential to stay in motion. Those who stand still over the ball and slowly go over their mental checklist will get

tight, which will restrict motion. All the planning for the stroke should be done before you address the ball. Almost all golfers go through the experience of "self-talk"—the mental checklist of all the swing motions we should or should not do. Self-talk takes time, and if it is done as you stand over and address the ball, it will produce tension and reduce motion. The way to produce your best swing is to review the motions you are trying to create, take a practice swing to "feel" the motion, and then try

to repeat that feel when you swing through the ball.

Most good players choose to start the swing with a forward press, which is a slight move with the hands and the right knee toward the target before actually starting the swing. This move will transfer some weight to the left foot and then rock back to the right foot. To make a good backswing you should shift about 80% of your weight to your back foot. This subtle forward-backward move is the easiest way to initiate the weight shift.

The Golf Swing

From a balanced address, swing the club back with the triangle formed by your arms and a line across your shoulders. The "center" of your body (the center is the middle of your chest) swings with the club. The left

At the top of the swing the player has created power by "winding up" the upper part of his body.

knee is starting to break toward the right knee while the weight of your body moves to the back foot. The wrists begin to "hinge" as a product of a proper grip. At the top of the swing your have created power by "winding up" the big mus-

The downswing is a natural unwinding of the power created and also includes the transfer of body weight from the back foot to the front foot...

The player has allowed the club to swing freely. This is called "releasing the club" and is demonstrated by the right forearm over the left forearm...

In the proper finish, almost all the player's weight is on the front foot, the spine is straight, the chest or "center" is facing the target, and the arms are relaxed.

Notice the hinging of the wrists. This is a product of the proper grip.

At the top of the swing, a) the shaft of the club points to the target, b) weight is on the back foot, and c) the player is in balance.

The backswing is started by swinging the clubhead away from the target with the arms and shoulders. This is called a "one piece" takeaway.

cles of your upper body. Notice that the "center" is facing directly away from your target, and weight has shifted to your back foot.

The change of direction from backswing to downswing is a natural unwinding and release of power you have created. The downswing is initiated by this natural unwinding as well as the weight transfer from back foot to front foot.

There are no tricks to solid contact. As you swing the club through the ball and toward the target, the ball merely gets in the way of a good swinging motion. The follow through is the grand finale of all the previous steps. The "center" has moved toward the target, the club has been fully swung and is held relaxed over the left shoulder, and almost all the weight is on the forward foot.

The downswing is initiated by the natural unwinding of the body and a weight shift from back foot to front.

In the follow through, the player is in balance facing the target.

Weight has transferred toward the front foot.

The player is swinging the clubhead freely toward the target.

You rotate your body away from the target on the backswing and then rotate the body toward the target on the forward swing. The length of your swing is a product of how flexible you are.

A good golf swing is smooth, rhythmical, and in balance. As in all sports you should be free of any tension or tightness. Grip pressure should be soft, and you should feel well balanced at address. You should never swing so fast that you lose your balance. To create a fluid feeling you should stay relaxed as you address the ball. Small pre-swings, called "the waggle," will help you feel the swing and keep you in motion.

The hinging of the wrist on the backswing and the unhinging of the wrist just after you hit the ball are natural actions. They result from the correct grip and soft-to-medium grip pressure. You will feel as if your right forearm is "crossing over" your left forearm on the follow through. Tension can restrict this action, which will result in loss of power and a weak shot to the right.

The swing is the continuous motion of the club head away from the target and then toward the target. The concept is to allow the swinging motion of the club to generate power and accuracy. You must trust your swing to achieve the best results.

Good players do not try to hit the ball. They try to create a series of good swings.

4

SAND PLAY

Sand bunkers are a strategic part of the game. Some bunkers are placed near the greens to create challenge for an approach shot, while others are alongside the fairways to challenge accuracy off the tee.

Sand bunkers are hazards, and the rules state you cannot remove any loose impediments, such as stones or leaves. You also are not allowed to "ground" the club (touch the club head to the sand) when you address the ball, so you should hold the club head an inch or two above the sand.

In the sand shot, the ball is positioned "forward" in the stance; the player will swing through a two-inch area of sand behind the ball.

The swing for the sand shot is no different from the regular swing. Because the sand acts like a cushion, the player must make a fairly full swing, even for a shot of a short distance.

The one trouble shot that intimidates most golfers is one from the greenside bunker. Players often go so far out of their way not to hit in them that they waste strokes elsewhere. The greenside bunker shot is not difficult but it does require a certain technique that is different from the standard golf shot. This technique was created by Gene Sarazen, who is one of the few players ever to win all four major championships.

To play the *greenside bunker shot*, use a sand wedge. This club is especially designed to have extra metal, called the "bounce," on the bottom of the club head. This design helps the club skim through but not dig too deeply into the sand. The grip and posture should be the same as in a regular shot from the grass. If the lie is good, open your stance by aligning the body to the left of the target. When you take your stance, dig your feet slightly into the sand. This will provide a good foundation and give you some feel for the texture of the sand. The club face will be aimed, or square, to the target (doing this makes the "bounce" design more effective). Swing the club through the sand so that it enters the sand about 1 1/2 to 2 inches behind the ball. In effect, you are swinging a sand divot out of the bunker. If the ball is anywhere in that divot it will fly softly onto the green. Because the sand acts as a cushion, the sand shot requires a swing that is fairly full. To vary the distance of the sand shot, vary how hard you swing. The distance the club enters the sand should always be about 1 1/2 to 2 inches and should not vary with the length of each shot.

The player is swinging through the sand. Both the divot of sand and the ball land on the green.

Dig your feet into the sand slightly when you take your stance. This will ensure sound balance and give you some idea of the texture of the sand.

In the sand shot, the ball is played forward in the stance.

The stance is slightly open.

As you play different golf courses you will notice that the texture of the sand will vary quite a bit. Some sand will be very light in color and soft, while other sand will be dark and coarse. Because the sand acts as a cushion in this shot, the texture of the sand will affect how far the ball flies. If the sand is soft the ball will come out softly; if the sand is coarse the ball will come out faster. Therefore in soft sand you need a fuller swing. Good players learn to adjust to these different conditions.

Occasionally the ball will be in a *buried lie.* To play from a buried lie, square the stance and

address the ball opposite your back foot. The club head will appear closed. This address position will insure a steep swing that will allow the club head to dig into the sand. The loft of the sand wedge as well as the downward action of the swing will pop the ball up out of the buried lie. The swing will feel choppy and there will be little or no follow through.

The *fairway bunker shot* is very different from the green-side bunker shot. In this shot you are trying to achieve some distance. Unlike the greenside bunker shot, the object is to hit the ball first and disrupt very little sand. This is a shot that

The clubface will be laid back. It will appear to be "open."

The swing should be smooth and unhurried.

The clubhead enters the sand $1 \frac{1}{2}$ inches behind the ball.

A divot of sand and the ball come out of the bunker.

Distance is determined by how hard you swing.

A full follow through will ensure a good shot.

should be played conservatively. If you hit a poor shot out of a fairway bunker the ball will probably land in the front part of the bunker and present an even more difficult next shot.

As in every shot there are two parts: the plan and the execution. The plan should be to select a club with enough loft to easily lift the ball over the front portion of the bunker. To execute, choke down on the club and address the ball more toward the back foot.

Very seldom should you try to hit a fairway wood out of a fairway bunker. It is a difficult shot and seldom does the reward outweigh the risk.

5

THE SHORT GAME

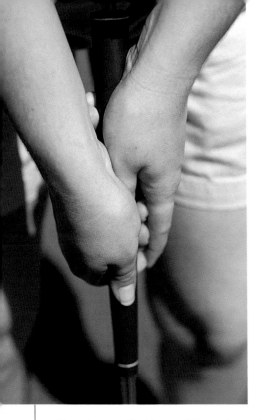

Putting

The art of putting has changed dramatically in the last few years. While there are a wide variety of recommended methods, there are a few fundamentals that all good players use.

The putting grip is different from the one used for full swings. The handle of the putter should be held much more in the palms so there is no wrist or hinge action. The palms of the hands should face each other and be square to the club face.

This lack of hand action will produce a pendulum-type putting stroke. You'll feel as if you are moving your arms and shoulders together. The size of the putting stroke should match the length of the putt. A short putt of 3 or 4 feet requires a short stroke, while a longer putt will require a longer stroke. Matching the size of the stroke to distance is a product of practice. The tempo of the stroke should be smooth and even.

In a good putting stroke the putting is swung by the triangle formed by the arms and a line across the shoulders; there is no hinging of the wrists, and the head stays still.

Determining the line of the putt. Putting greens are not perfectly flat like a pool table. The natural rolls on the green will cause the ball to curve downhill. This is called the "break" of the putt. The amount of break is determined by the severity of the slope and the speed of the green. As the severity of the slope and speed of the green increase, so does the amount of break. You need to allow for this natural break and aim to a spot that is uphill from the hole.

The key to being a good putter is to be able to control the distance of the putt. Ideally every putt you hit should either go in the hole or have enough

speed to roll about one foot past the hole.

When you have a short putt of a few feet that you expect to make, hit the ball firmly enough to reach the back of the cup. Nothing is more frustrating than leaving a 3-foot putt short. Striking the putt so that it reaches the back of the hole will do three things:

a. Eliminate or lessen the amount of break;

b. Lessen the influence small imperfections, such as pebbles or sand, have on the roll of the putt;

c. Reduce the chances of leaving the putt short.

A good putting routine consists of the following steps:

1. Determine the line of the putt.

2. Work on speed by "visualizing" the putt.

3. Make a few practice strokes, trying to match the size of your stroke with the distance you are trying to achieve.

4. Square the putter face to the line. This may sound simple but it is tricky because we stand parallel to the line, not behind it. To consistently square the blade, first line up the putt behind the ball so you can draw an imaginary line along the grass to the hole. Pick out a spot (this could be a discolored piece of grass, old ball mark, etc.) that is only a foot or two in front of your ball on this imaginary line. Place the putter behind the ball and square it to the "spot."

5. Make a smooth stroke.

6. Keep the body still.

In the chip shot, the player shortens the club by choking up. In this shot the ball is positioned slightly back in the stance.

The Chip Shot

A chip shot is a very short shot that you play when you are 2 to 30 feet from the hole. The first step is to visualize how the ball will fly, land on the green, and eventually roll toward the hole. This plan should include allowing for the natural break. It should also be as much like a putt as possible, so normally

The chip shot is similar to a putting stroke. There is no wrist hinge or weight transfer. The size of the stroke is determined by picturing the shot and applying a stroke of the right length.

you would use a middle iron (4, 5 or 6) if you are 2 to 6 feet off the green, and a more lofted iron if you are farther from the green. Other considerations in choosing the correct iron for chipping are wind, speed of the green, and distance to the pin.

When chipping into the wind select a less lofted club, such as a 5 iron instead of a 7 iron, so that the wind does not affect the ball as much and the ball easily reaches the hole. If the wind is behind you, select a club with a little more loft to prevent the ball from sliding past the hole.

Putting greens vary in texture and length and therefore the ball will roll at varying speeds. If the green is "fast" you should choose a club with more loft, such as a 7 iron rather than a 5 iron, so the ball does not slide by the hole. If the grass on the green is longer than usual the ball will not roll quickly as it normally would. In this case use a 5 iron instead of a 7 iron to ensure you reach the hole.

Distance to the pin is also a factor in choosing the correct iron for chipping. If you are 6 feet off the green and the pin is fairly close, use a lofted 7 or 8 iron. When the pin is on the far side of the green, the correct choice is a 5 or 6 iron.

Other considerations in choosing the correct club include whether you are uphill or downhill of the hole. If you are uphill, choose a less lofted club to ensure you reach the hole. If you are downhill, use a less lofted club so the ball does not go too far past the hole.

If the area around the green is bare, you may use a putter when off the green. The putter then is referred to a "Texas wedge" as this is a very popular shot on some dry Texas courses.

To execute the chip shot you should choke up on the club, position the ball just right of center, and make a short swing. The size of the swing should increase as the distance from the hole increases.

The key to being successful around the greens is to visualize the easiest possible play and then execute it with confidence.

In the pitch shot, the ball is positioned just right of center in the stance.

The Pitching Wedge

A pitching wedge is used for most shots that are longer than 30 feet from the green yet shorter than a full 9 iron. That distance is from about 10 to 100 yards.

As in all shots, start by making a plan and picturing where you want the ball to land and roll toward the pin. The next step is to gauge the distance. The size of the swing should match the length of the shot. In a short shot of 30 yards, you

The pitch shot is a "mini swing"; there is a some hinging of the wrists and very little weight transfer. The size of the swing is determined by imagination. The player has to visualize the shot and then create the proper swing.

would swing the club head a little short of waist-high on the backswing, then waist-high on the follow through. On a longer shot of 50 yards, swing the club head a little more than waist-high on the backswing and waist-high on the follow through.

A good trick is to use your imagination and picture yourself standing in the face of a clock with your head at the 12 and your feet at the 6. Take the normal address position and then swing the club head from

7 to 5 for a 30 yard shot, 9 to 3 for a 60 yard shot, and 10 to 2 for an 80 yard shot. Each player has to determine his or her distance for each shot, and that takes practice.

The same fundamentals that were covered in the full swing apply to the wedge shot. You must have a good grip and posture, a smooth swinging action, the club moving with the center of your body, and a good finish, facing the target with weight on the forward foot.

A quick note for more advanced players on strokes played with a pitching wedge: If the ball is sitting down in the grass, you should position it slightly back in your stance. This will somewhat decrease the loft and create a lower shot, but it will create a steeper downswing, allowing the club head to swing into the ball. The downward action of the club and the loft of the club will lift the ball from a difficult lie.

In the flop shot, the ball is positioned forward in the stance.

The Flop Shot

The flop shot is a short, high shot that lands softly on the green and has very little roll. This shot is played over bunkers and hazards. The correct club is the sand wedge, as it has the most loft of any club in the set.

To play this shot:

Open your stance (your feet, hips, and shoulders are aimed to the left of your target).

The ball position should be left center.

Make a big slow swing and keep your arms moving.

Advanced Short Game Techniques

The bladed sand wedge or fairway wood shot. On occasion the ball will settle down in the grass just off the green or will roll up against that long grass. The long grass will be between the club face and the ball, making it impossible to strike the ball cleanly. If you try to play a standard chip shot in

Notice the open stance. A line across the player's toes would be left of the target.

The player makes a big, slow swing and keeps the arms moving.

this situation, you will probably catch the grass before the ball and only hit it a few feet or hit the ball too cleanly and skip it across the green. A good method to successfully play this stroke is to choose a sand wedge, then address the leading edge of the club face to the equator or middle of the ball. The swing itself should be identical to a putting stroke; same grip, same ball position and the same size stroke. The leading edge of the sand wedge will cut right through the grass, hitting the ball at the equator, and the ball will roll surprisingly like a putt. The same concept can be employed with a fairway wood. We have all watched the remarkable results Tiger Woods has achieved with this stroke. Tiger simply putts the ball out of the long grass with a 3 wood.

The long greenside bunker shot. Good players agree that the most difficult shot in golf is a long bunker shot, with 25 or 30 yards to the hole. The standard method is to use a sand wedge, open the stance, swing through an area behind the ball, and then take a full swing. Because the sand acts as a cushion, the ball is usually left well short of the hole. Or, sometimes players overcorrect and sail the ball over the green.

There are two modifications you can use to make this difficult stroke a little easier. First, after you take your stance, move about an inch farther away from the ball. This will ensure a shallower swing and will prevent the club head from digging too deeply into the sand.

Second, use an iron other than a sand wedge, such as an 8 or 9 iron. Use the same technique as for the standard sand shot: open the stance, and swing through the area behind the ball, removing a cushion of sand and the ball from the bunker. Since the 8 or 9 iron has less loft, the ball will go farther. This technique requires some experimentation to get a feel for distance.

How to play from the hardpan. Hardpan is hard packed ground with little or no grass. There are a variety of methods to play from the hardpan, depending upon the type of stroke required. If you have a clear line to the pin, the correct club is a putter, and the stroke is played as if you were on the green. If you need some loft on the shot use a pitching wedge, and play the ball back in your stance. Playing the ball back in the stance creates a slightly lower ball flight but will ensure solid contact.

Occasionally the ball will be behind a sand bunker. You will need a high shot that stops quickly. To achieve that result, play it exactly as you would a standard sand shot: open the stance, swing through an area behind the ball, and follow through.

All three of these methods require imagination and practice, but can save you many strokes along the way.

6

TROUBLE SHOTS

There are many types of trouble shot. Here are a few suggestions to cover the most common ones.

Sidehill, downhill, and uphill lies. Golf courses are seldom if ever flat. When faced with a lie that is uneven, you generally have to make a minor adjustment in your address position. The best and most accurate way to gauge that adjustment is to take a practice swing in the particular situation and note where the club brushes the grass. If the club head brushes the grass nearer the back foot, move the ball back in your stance. If the club brushes the grass more toward your front foot, move the ball forward. Seldom does a player have a purely sidehill or uphill lie. This method takes all the factors into account as the practice swing is the rehearsal for the actual shot.

On the uphill lie, the ball is placed about center in the stance.

Make an extra effort to follow through. This is a little more difficult, as you have to swing up the hill.

the effect of closing the club face and decreasing loft. For this reason, use a more lofted club than if the ball were in the fairway. Even if there is a great deal of distance left, the first consideration should be to use a lofted club to get the ball out of the rough. In long grass around the green, use a lofted club such as a pitching or sand wedge. In all shots from long grass allow the loft of the club to lift the ball.

Long grass will limit the amount of control you have over the ball. The moisture

A general rule of thumb on uneven lies is to position the ball nearer the higher foot on downhill lies and about center on uphill lies. On sidehill lies, position the ball left center (as you normally would). If the ball position is higher than your feet, the ball will pull left; if it is below your feet you will hit the ball straight or a little to the right. You will also have to adjust your club selection on the uphill and downhill lies. An uphill lie will provide a higher flight than normal. As you take your stance the club will automatically have increased loft.

Therefore you have to use at least one more club. If you are playing an uphill lie and have a normal 6 iron distance you should choose a 4 or 5 iron.

If you are playing a downhill stroke, the club will automatically have decreased loft. Therefore if you have a 5 iron distance you should play the stroke with a 6 iron. The steeper the hill the more of an adjustment you will have to make.

Long grass. This is difficult to play from as the grass will get between the club head and the ball. Long grass will also have

In the downhill shot, position the ball more toward your back foot and swing the clubhead down the hill.

43

from the grass gets between the ball and the club face and produces a "flyer." The moisture reduces the amount of spin on the ball so it flies like a knuckleball in baseball. The ball will normally carry farther and roll more than normal. The best way to play a flyer is to use at least one less club (a 7 iron instead of a 6 iron) and aim at the front and center of the green.

Getting out of trouble spots on the course. Often players get into trouble and compound their difficulties by trying to play a miracle shot to get out. The best approach is to play the shot you know you can play, not the shot Tiger Woods would try. When hitting over a tree, take one club extra. If you think you can just clear the tree with a 7 iron, take an 8 or 9 iron. If you think a 5 iron will just stay under those branches, hit a 4 or 3 iron. This approach simply gives you the benefit of the doubt and will take pressure off your shot. It also puts the percentages on your side. This is the chess side of golf, and it is as important as hitting the ball well.

7

ADVANCED
SHOT-MAKING

To hit the ball higher than normal, position the ball two or three inches forward and open the stance slightly.

As you develop as a player you will want to learn new skills. Having the ability to hit the ball high or low, or intentionally curve the ball will enable you to adjust to weather conditions and play out of difficult situations.

To hit a *low shot* select a club with less loft. If you are at a distance that requires a 7 iron, choose a 5 or 6 iron. The ball is normally addressed a little forward in the stance with a 5 iron. For the intentional low shot, address the ball back in the stance about 2–3 inches. This will decrease the loft of the club, creating a low trajectory. The swing itself should not be full. A three-quarter backswing with a low follow-through will produce a low shot. This is a valuable shot on those windy days or when you have to keep the ball under tree branches.

To hit the ball high over a tree you should choose a club with loft. A good rule of thumb is to always select a club with a little more loft than you think you need. To hit the ball high, open the stance slightly and address the ball forward in the stance 2–3 inches. This will increase the loft of the club. Use a full swing with a complete follow through.

Intentionally curving the ball is useful for playing around trouble, shortcutting a dogleg, or playing to a pin that is located on the far left or right of the green.

To play a shot left to right, open your stance so an imaginary line across your toes is well left of your target, and then open the club face slightly. This will automatically create an outside-in swing pattern, producing a left-to-right flight. Advanced players will try not to "release" the club by keeping the heel of the club ahead of the toe of the club.

To play a shot right to left, close your stance so an imaginary line across your toes is well to the right of your target and then close the club face slightly. This will automatically create an inside-out swing pattern producing a right-to-left flight. Advanced players will try to aggressively "release" the club by rotating the toe of the club past the heel.

Intentionally curving the ball when playing approach shots to the green is called "*working" the ball.* The most effective way to work the ball to a pin that is on the extreme right or left of the green is to aim at the center of the green and then inten-tionally curve it to the pin. If the ball does curve, it will be next to the pin; if not, it will be in the center of the green.

The 3/4 shot. During the course of the round you will have many situations where you will have trouble assessing what club to use for an approach shot. You may be 135 yards to the pin and know your normal 6 iron carries 130 yards and the

A full follow through will help in producing an intentionally high shot.

The three-quarter shot is played by choking down on the handle one or two inches and shortening both the backswing and follow through.

5 iron carries 140 yards. Since the 6 iron, even if well struck, cannot reach the green, you need to shorten the distance you hit the 5 iron. To take a few yards off the 5 iron, choke up on the club about 2 inches and swing as if you were playing a long pitch shot. Your hands should reach 10 o'clock on the backswing and 2 o'clock on the follow through. This takes some feel but is a great project for a practice session.

8

ETIQUETTE

A young girl doing warm-up stretching exercises

Golf etiquette is the way golfers act and dress at the golf course. Good golf etiquette will not lower your score but it will make your golf experience and that of others playing with you more enjoyable.

Dress. Many golf courses have dress codes that consist of comfortable clothing you probably already have in your closet.

Men and boys should wear:

Collared shirts;

Pants or shorts within 3" of the knee;

Spikeless golf shoes, rubber-soled shoes, or sneakers.

Jeans, tank tops, and T-shirts are not appropriate.

Women and girls should wear:

Collared shirts or a "dressy" T-shirt;

Pants, skirts, or shorts within 3" of the knee;

Spikeless golf shoes, rubber-soled shoes, or sneakers.

Jeans and halter tops are not appropriate.

Arrive early at the golf course. At most courses you call ahead for a "starting" or "tee" time. Arrive at the golf course about an hour before that time so that you can check in at the pro shop, pay green fees, and, most importantly, warm up at the driving range with some practice balls. Check in with the "starter" at least 10 minutes

before your assigned time. The starter will often give players information such as the local rules, cart policies, etc.

A good warm-up stretch. It is a good idea to do some stretching before playing. This will increase your flexibility as well as reduce the chances of a pulled muscle. A favorite exercise is to put a club behind your back and rotate your body similarly to the way you would during your golf swing. Assume a stance similar to your normal address position. Rotate to your backswing position and hold that position for 10 seconds. You will feel the "wind-up" that will create power. Then rotate your body to your follow-through position and again hold it for 10 seconds. It is not how fast or how many times you stretch but rather how fully you stretch. As in all stretching, do it slowly. You will gradually increase your flexibility, which in turn will increase your distance.

Warm-up shots. The best way to warm up is to start with short shots using a pitching wedge. Hit the first few with the goal of solid contact. Now pick a target. Gradually hit some longer irons, starting with an 8 iron, then a 5 iron. Next, pull out your driver, trying to picture the tee shot you hope to hit on the first tee. This practice session should be a rehearsal for that tee shot. Review your fundamentals: grip, posture, address, and a smooth swinging motion. End the warm-up with a few short wedge shots so you leave the practice tee feeling confident about the game you are about to play.

First Tee Etiquette. On the first tee:

Introduce yourself if you are paired with strangers.

Identify the ball you are playing.

Play the appropriate tees. There are normally three sets of tee markers on the teeing ground.

These different color tee markers vary the length of the course.

Red is short yardage.

White is medium yardage.

Blue is long yardage.

You should select the course length that provides a reasonable challenge but, most importantly, one that is short enough so you can enjoy your game.

A young woman repairing a ball mark. The ball mark should be pried up until the depression is gone and the area of the green is flat.

General Course Etiquette.

Be ready to hit when it is your turn.

Yell "fore" if a ball you hit has even the slightest chance of hitting someone.

Stand to the side and slightly behind the player who is hitting the ball (see "On-the-Green Etiquette").

The player who is farthest away plays first.

Pace of play. The game of golf should be played at a reasonable pace, which is about four hours for an 18-hole round. To keep the game moving:

Minimize your practice swings.

Be ready to hit when it's your turn.

Proceed to your ball as soon as it is safe to do so.

You may hit "out of turn" if it is safe to do so. This is called "ready golf."

Try to keep up with the group ahead of your group.

Pick up after "double par" (twice the par of the hole) and move on to the next hole.

Care of the course. True golfers try to leave the course in better condition than they found it, by replacing all divots, fixing ball marks (ball marks are small indentations on the green made by the impact of the ball landing), raking sand bunkers and showing care for the general condition of the course.

On-the-Green Etiquette

Mark your ball by placing a small coin or ball marker behind it.

Repair ball marks on the green (yours and one other). Repair a ball mark by using a tee or a divot tool to pry up the indentation made by the impact of ball. After you pry it up, tap down the area with a putter head to restore it to its original condition.

Avoid walking in your own line or the line of your playing partners. (The "line" is an imaginary path on the green directly between the ball and the hole.)

The player farthest from the hole putts first.

You should be looking at your putt when other players are putting so you are ready when it's your turn.

Leave the green immediately after the hole has been completed.

A young man raking the bunker after he has played from it

A young woman marking her ball. A small coin should be placed behind the ball and then the ball can be lifted and cleaned.

Golf Cart Etiquette

Become familiar with operating instructions and warnings on the cart.

Golf carts should never be close to greens or tees.

Observe local golf course rules regarding where you may drive the cart.

Around the green, park at the exit toward the next tee. This will save time.

Courtesy and common sense.
Golf is a social game, usually played in a group of three other people. Everyone in the foursome should have the opportunity to play without any unnecessary interference. The etiquette suggestions in this chapter cover most golf course protocol, but the single most important ingredient is common sense. Suggestions like staying still when one of the other players swings or keeping pace with the group ahead of you are normal courtesies that increase everyone's enjoyment.

Safety. Occasionally you may encounter lightning on the golf course. When this happens seek a building protected against lightning, a large unprotected building, or automobiles and shelters in low lying areas. Avoid open fields, isolated trees, and water.

9 ▶

POINTERS
FOR YOUNG
GOLFERS

A group lesson

Children can start playing golf at an early age. The trick is to find equipment that is not too heavy or too long.

Children should use equipment that is designed and fit especially for them. Cutting down adult clubs will not produce clubs that fit a child. First, the balance of the club will change dramatically. Second, the flex of the club will become much stiffer. Beginners, and especially children, need shafts that are flexible. The best way to acquire children's golf clubs is to find a golf shop that carries junior equipment. Just like adults, children need to be measured for the proper grip size and club length.

Children love to imitate. They should find a player with a great swing and try to make the same swing. It's fun and it works! The technical funda-

Young players taking instruction

mentals in chapters 3, 4, and 5 are the same. The only difference may be in how they hold the club. The best grip for children (and adults) with small hands is the ten-finger grip. When they get to be mid-teens they can switch to the Vardon or interlocking grip if they choose.

A great way for children to learn is to mimic the grip, posture, and swinging motion of their favorite golfer, such as Annika Sorenstam or David Duval. If they start out with good basics, the game will come easily.

A few suggestions that will always help are: stay in balance (sometime children swing so hard they cannot maintain their balance); swing the clubhead (feel the weight of the head of the club as you swing); at the top of the backswing the back

POINTERS FOR YOUNG GOLFERS

Young players taking instuction

should face the target; at the follow through the chest should face the target. It is easiest to learn if you are having fun. Be creative and invent competitions in the practice areas. Putting and chipping contests and aiming at different targets on the driving range or in your backyard go a long way toward learning fundamentals.

When playing on the course, try to hit solid golf shots. Until skills are developed, you really should not worry about score.

The best advice to getting started in golf is: imitate the stars and have fun!

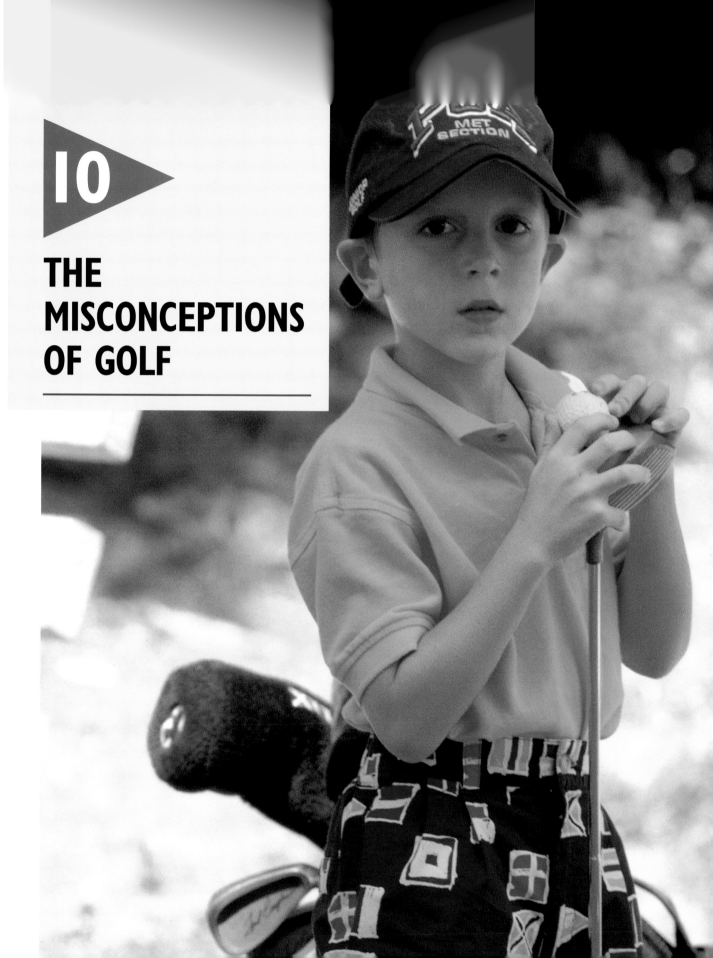

10

THE MISCONCEPTIONS OF GOLF

A full follow through on a bunker shot will ensure good results.

There is no shortage of advice in the game of golf. Well-meaning friends often offer suggestions about the game that not only do not help us improve but actually make us worse players. These suggestions are "The Misconceptions of Golf." A few of these misconceptions are:

Keep your head down. This is probably the most-often given piece of bad advice. Once you hear this you will probably bury your chin into your chest, ruining your posture. Establishing and maintaining good posture will allow for a free swinging motion.

Four players waiting to tee off

Keep the left arm straight. The golf swing should be free flowing. Trying to keep the left arm straight will increase tension and reduce motion. The left arm will be long or extended on the backswing, just as the right arm will be long or extended on the follow through, but at no time is either arm stiff.

Pull down with the left hand. Both hands swing the club. There really is no pulling or pushing. The hands work together.

Keep your head perfectly still. This will restrict motion. Your head should move a little during the swing as you transfer weight back and forward.

The Don'ts. Very often, well-meaning friends will tell you what to do or what not to do just as you are about to swing. The fear of doing something wrong will increase tension and decrease motion. In order to improve, a golfer must learn what to do.

There are many other misconceptions in golf. The best way to improve your game is to learn the fundamentals and stick to them.

IMAGINATION

The thrill of a good shot

Tiger Woods is certainly one of the most imaginative players in the world today. We have seen Tiger putt from just off the green with a fairway wood with amazing results. A good imagination in golf is a strong asset.

You use your imagination to visualize the shot you are about to play. Look down the fairway and picture your ideal tee shot—what it will look like before you actually play it. Then try to picture the flight of your approach shot to the green. Will it be high or low? Will it land short of the green and roll onto the green or will it land softly on the green and stop quickly? Finally imagine or picture the putt as it starts to the left of the hole and then breaks toward the cup and finally drops in for a birdie (one under par for the hole)!

Visualizing the shot before you play it sends your brain a clear message of what you are trying to do. The more clearly you understand the task (the golf shot you are trying to play), the more likely you will be successful.

Imagination is also the key to club selection and playing the "best" shot. The best shot is simply the one you feel most comfortable playing. You can use your imagination to visualize a few different ways to play a particular stroke and then judge which is best for you. For instance, your ball is lying 10 yards off the green on bare, hard ground. The area between your ball and the green has little or no grass. Normally from this distance you would use a 9 iron or pitching wedge. As you visualize your options you realize you have at least three choices:

1. The standard pitch shot.

2. A chip shot with a 7 or 8 iron.

3. You could even putt the ball (because the ball would roll on the bare ground much as it would on the green).

The best shot is the one you have the most confidence in. Create a good positive picture and you will get the results you want.

12

COURSE
MANAGEMENT

Course management is the ability to use your golf skills to produce the best possible score. The first step to managing your game is to honestly assess your skills. Recognizing both strengths and weaknesses will help you play smart and also identify areas that need improvement.

Golf is a lot like chess. You plan your first stroke (move) with the idea of making the next stroke as easy as possible. The classic example of this is when you are playing short of a hazard and hitting the ball in position for an approach to the green. You should play the lay-up shot to a part of the fairway that is level and at a distance from the green that you are good at. You have a much better chance of success if you have an 80-yard approach shot from the fairway than a 30-yard approach from the deep rough.

Another step to good course management is to get the percentages in your favor by playing smart shots and not taking unnecessary chances. For instance, you have driven the ball 200 yards off the tee, in the right rough on a 420-yard hole. The ball is nestled down in the grass. If you try to hit a fairway wood out of that lie, which you are unlikely to do successfully, you will probably be 40 yards short of the green. If you use a 7 iron for the same shot, at which you will probably be successful, you will be 80 yards short of the green. In both cases you will have a relatively short wedge shot to the green. The difference in accuracy between a 40-yard and an 80-yard wedge for your third stroke is minimal. By using the 7 iron instead of the fairway wood you have put the percentages for success in your favor. You should never take a chance if it will not save a stroke.

Identifying the Lie

How the ball sits in the grass is one of the most overlooked yet extremely important aspects of course management. When the ball is sitting up on the grass, as if on a small tee, it is very easy to address the ball so that the middle of the club face is squarely behind the middle of the ball. If you make a good swing you will achieve solid contact.

If the ball is sitting down in the grass or in any type of depression, you cannot easily match the middle of the club

A young girl hitting a chip shot

face to the middle of the ball. You then have to make some adjustments, because if you make a good swing the club face will contact the top of the ball, resulting in an unsolid hit. First, select a club with a little extra loft. This will help get the ball up. Second, play the ball back in the stance. This will make it easier to match the middle of the club face to the middle of the ball at address as well as create a slightly steeper downswing. This steeper down-swing will drive the club head into the turf. The downward pressure of the club head and

A young player making a full swing

the loft of the club will produce a solid, lofted shot. Remember: The key is to be able to match the middle of the club face easily to the middle of the ball at address. If the middle of the ball is below the middle of the club face at address, choose a more lofted club and move the ball back in your stance.

Examples of good course management:

1. Play the shot you are most comfortable playing. For instance, if your choice is to use a fairway wood or a long iron, choose the club that gives you the most confidence. In most cases playing a 7 wood is a lot easier than a 3 or 4 iron.

2. Play the shot you know you can hit. We are always faced with choices when we play. Should I try to hit over the water? Should I aim at the pin that is just behind the sand bunker? The answer is to play the shot that you know you can hit, leaving some margin for error. Never play a shot that requires a 100% solid hit to achieve your goal.

Keep clubs and other golf equipment well maintained.

67

It's a good idea to line up the putt from behind the ball to best determine the line.

3. The tee shot sets up your game. If you naturally slice or fade your drives, tee up on the right side of the tee and aim at the left side of the fairway. If the ball goes straight you'll be on the left side of the fairway. If it slices or fades a little the ball it will be dead center. If you've sliced it a lot you'll still be in the right side of the fairway. On a day you are having difficulty controlling your direction with the driver, try a 3 or 5 wood off the tee. You may lose a little distance but the advantages of accuracy more than outweigh the loss of distance.

4. On approach shots to the green it is generally best to aim to the center of the green rather than to aim at a flagstick that is behind a bunker.

5. When putting, try to gauge the distance so that your first putt is close enough for an easy second putt. If you have a long putt with a lot of break, it is best to play a little more break than you see. This way the ball will be curving toward the hole, not away from it as it slows down.

13

TOURNAMENT
PLAY

As your skills develop and scores become lower, you may play in tournaments. Whether it is the Junior Club Championship or the U.S. Open, you will feel some pressure. Absolutely no one is exempt. There are some important do's and don't's along the way.

Two players preparing to play

Young players signing their scorecards after they have played in a tournament

Do be prepared. In your golf bag carry a rainsuit, an umbrella, an extra towel, a rain hat, a few extra gloves, your favorite brand of golf ball (properly marked), coins or ball markers in your pocket to mark your ball on the green (I use a quarter to mark my ball when I have a long putt and a dime near the hole), a few granola bars, and whatever else you think you might need.

Do play a practice round. Even if you have played the course before, it is important to play a practice round the day before to gauge the speed of the greens and get a feel for how the course is playing in general.

Do eat. The first-tee jitters can ruin an appetite but it really is important to have a good meal full of carbohydrates before you play. It is also a good idea to carry a granola bar in your bag to eat during the round. If you warm up in the practice area and then experience some delays you may be walking up the 18th fairway six hours after you last ate.

Do drink water on the way to the course and during the round.

71

Do breathe. When we are in stressful situations we breathe short, quick breaths. Try to take a deep breath and breathe out slowly. It will do wonders for your nerves.

Do your pre-shot routine. Many players spend too much time in the address position standing still over the ball when they are under pressure. The pre-shot routine in a tournament should be identical to the routine you use in normal play.

Do arrive early to the course. Give yourself plenty of time to get to the course to relax, eat, practice, and allow for some type of delay.

Do hold the golf club with a light grip. Tournament tension often equals squeezing the club too tightly.

Don't drink caffeinated coffee or soda.

Don't eat candy bars or chocolate for quick energy.

Don't rush.

Do enjoy yourself. These tournaments are fun!

Remember that everyone in the tournament is going to hit good and bad shots. Hit it, chase it, and stay cool. You never know when a good round is going to pop up.

14

MAJOR
COMPETITIONS

There are a variety of major competitions for all players.

The American Junior Golf Association (AJGA), headquartered in Roswell, Georgia, hosts tournaments for juniors under 18 throughout the United States with a final championship at the end of the season.

The United States Golf Association (USGA), headquartered in Far Hills, New Jersey, hosts tournaments for men and women, young and old. The U.S. Junior Amateur and U.S. Girls' Junior are competitions for young players under 18 years old.

The USGA conducts the U.S. Open, Women's U.S. Open, U.S. Amateur, U.S. Women's Amateur, Mid-Amateurs for men and women, a Public Links Championship for men and women, as well as a Senior Open for those 50 and older.

The USGA also conducts two international amateur competitions: The Walker Cup is composed of a team of the best American male amateurs who compete against a European team. The competitions are played in odd-numbered years and the venues alternate between courses in the United States and in Europe. The

Curtis Cup is a similar competition with teams composed of the best amateur female competitors.

The Royal and Ancient Golf Club of Edinburgh conducts similar competitions for golfers in Great Britain. The "British Open" is the oldest and, many players feel, the most revered tournament in the world.

The Ladies' Professional Golf Association (LPGA), headquartered in Daytona Beach, Florida, hosts a full schedule of 25 tournaments with its Championship being the highlight. The major tournaments for Lady Professional players are the LPGA Championship, the U.S. Women's Open, the British Women's Open, and the Dinah Shore Invitational. The LPGA also conducts the

Solheim Cup, an invitational team competition against a European team of female professionals. The teams alternate venues and play in even-numbered years.

The PGA of America, headquartered in Palm Beach Gardens, Florida, hosts a full schedule of 30 tournaments, with its championship being the highlight. The major tournaments for men professional golfers are the U.S. Open, the British Open, the PGA Championship, and the Masters. The PGA also conducts the Ryder Cup, an invitational competition against a European team of male professionals. Like the Solheim Cup, the teams alternate venues but play in odd-numbered years.

15

THE RULES
OF GOLF

Golf has been played since the mid 1400s. For the first three hundred years there were no rules. In 1744, the Company of Gentlemen Golfers, Edinburgh, Scotland, wrote "The Original Rules of Golf." The three basic ideas behind the original rules were:

1. Play the ball as it lies.

2. Play the course as you find it.

3. When you cannot do either of these, do what is fair.

These ideas are still the foundation of the rules to this day. If you follow the spirit of these original rules you will be an honest golfer.

Golf is the only game with no umpires or referees. Golfers play by The Rules of Golf which are established by the United States Golf Association and the Royal and Ancient Golf Club of St. Andrews, Scotland. In tournament play, a rules official will help interpret the rules, but in both tournament and non-tournament play it is up to the player to make decisions regarding the rules.

Scoring: There are two types of play: match play and stroke play. Match play was the original form of play. In match play you play against one opponent and compete hole by hole. If player A scores a 6 on the first hole and player B scores a 4, then player B is "one up." The final score is determined by who wins the most holes. If player B has won 6 more holes than player A after 13 holes, then player A wins the match 6 and 5. Player B is 6 holes "up" with only 5 to play.

The other method of play is stroke or medal play. The medal score is simply the amount of strokes a player takes for the round of golf. This is the style of competition used most in professional tournaments. You play the course as do fellow competitors and the lowest score wins.

Rules. USGA Rule 13-1 says: "The ball shall be played as it lies, except as provided in the Rules." Following are a few circumstances where the ball is not played as it lies.

Lost ball. If you lose your ball you replay from the original position under a penalty of one stroke plus the original stroke.

Unplayable ball. If your ball lands in a spot that you can't play from, you may move the ball under penalty of one stroke. You are the sole judge to determine if the ball is playable. You have three options; choose the one that gives you the best relief.

1. You may drop a ball within two club lengths of the spot where the ball lay, but not nearer the hole.

2. Or, you may drop a ball behind the spot where the ball lay, keeping that spot between you and the hole. There is no limit to how far back you can go.

3. Or you can exercise the same penalty for a lost ball, which is stroke and distance.

Water hazards. A water hazard (yellow stakes) is any sea, lake, pond, river, ditch, or anything similar. If you choose not to play from the hazard you may either drop another ball behind the hazard, under penalty of one stroke, keeping the point where the ball last crossed the margin of the hazard between yourself and the hole, or use the same procedure for a lost ball. Some water hazards are lateral water hazards (red stakes). If your ball goes in a lateral hazard you may drop a ball within two club lengths of where the ball last crossed the margin of the hazard, not nearer the hole, or a point on the opposite side of the hazard the same distance from the hole. You may also use the regular water hazard options. The penalty is one stroke.

Man-made objects. You get relief from man-made objects with no penalty. If your ball comes to rest next to a building (an immovable obstruction) you may take the nearest relief not nearer to the hole. If the ball comes to rest under a bench (a movable obstruction) you may move the bench.

Unfair conditions. There are some natural conditions that occur that are unfair and the rules provide relief.

1. "Ground Under Repair" is an area that is being worked on by the golf maintenance staff. This area is normally marked and defined by a painted white line.

2. A hole made by a burrowing animal.

3. Casual water, which is an accumulation of water.

In all three situations drop the ball within one club length of the nearest spot that provides relief, not nearer the hole. There is no penalty.

It is a good idea to buy a USGA Rules Book and carry it in your golf bag.

16

PRACTICE
DRILLS

Practice should be productive and fun. To make it productive, first analyze what area of your game needs the most improvement. Count how many drives you hit that end up in the fairway, how many of your irons reach the green, how many putts you use per round, etc. Find the weakest area and then dedicate yourself to improvement. All practice should have a goal. It may be a higher percentage of 10-foot putts, or more drives in the fairway. On a notepad chart your progress and the swing corrections you have made. This will prevent you from following the wrong path and will provide valuable feedback.

The "toe-up/toe-up" drill

At the top of this mini swing, the toe of the club is pointing up.

You can make practice fun by creating "games." Ideally you can practice with a friend and organize competitions. Who can make the most short putts in a row, the most balls out of ten from the bunker, reach the most fairways out of ten off the tee, etc. This type of practice provides some competition and helps you identify your own strengths and weaknesses.

We practice to improve both our score and our enjoyment. This requires the ability to change and, most importantly, to think. Limit the time of your practice sessions to the time you can be strong mentally and physically. Many practice ses-

sions do not produce the results they should because the player hit too many practice balls, got tired, and fell back into old bad habits.

Instruction and information combined with intelligent practice are the ingredients to a better golf game!

Practice Drills

Long game: A good practice drill is the "Toe-Up/Toe-Up Drill." Using a wedge, make half swings with the hands swinging about waist high. On this length backswing, the toe of the club should point up, and on the

forward swing the toe of the club should also point up. A normal weight transfer will allow you to release your back foot so the right heel is off the ground and you are balancing on your front foot.

If the toe of the club is not "up" on the backswing and follow through, look for corrections starting with the grip and then the alignment. This is an excellent way to start a warm-up session or a good drill to go through when you are having trouble with your game. It is easier to correct a swing flaw with this short swing than with a full swing.

At the finish of this mini-swing, the toe of the club is pointing up.

The split grip. This is a terrific way to practice if you are trying to correct hitting the ball to the right.

The split grip drill. This drill is particularly good for players who want to correct a slice. In this drill you can use any club in the bag. After you establish your grip, slide your bottom hand down the grip so you have about a 3-inch gap between your hands. By separating your hands, the bottom hand will normally become a little more aggressive and you will be able to feel the "release." The release of the club is a natural result of the force created by the swing-

ing action of the club. Very often players do not allow that action to happen because their grip is too tight or they have established an incorrect swing pattern. As with all shots, grip pressure should be light. By using the split grip drill you will more easily square the club head to the target, rather than leave it open.

The sand drill is a surefire way to become a better greenside bunker player. Draw a 3-inch circle in the sand bunker, then address the circle as if the ball were in the middle of it. Swing through the circle and try to splash all the sand out of the bunker. After you have done that a few times put a ball in the center of the circle. Once again swing through the sand and try to splash the circle of sand and the ball out of the bunker.

The coin drill for putting is a good drill for alignment. This is particularly good if you are having trouble "seeing" the line when you address the putt. Find a 10-foot putt with no break. Line it up from behind and

place a coin directly in that line halfway between you and the hole. Now address the ball, look down the line, and see if the coin appears to have moved. If so, your perception of the line has become distorted. Practice lining up at the coin and rolling the ball over it. Soon you will be lining up and focusing on the line correctly.

The "No-Peek" drill is a good putting and chipping drill. Practice hitting putts and other short shots, keeping your head still and never looking up. Then try to guess where the ball finished, right or left or long or short of the hole. Remaining still and not looking up at all eliminates the possibility of compensating for misalignment. This will give you some valuable feedback.

Most players reach the hole on only about half their putts. During a practice round, when you are not concerned with score, challenge yourself to see if you can play all 18 holes without leaving one putt short of the hole.

17

TRAINING
DEVICES

Use of teaching devices can enhance your practice sessions.

A heavy bag of sand or an "impact bag" as shown here can help you improve your impact position and your ability to hit the ball.

Set up as you normally would and substitute the impact bag for your ball.

Take a normal swing, allowing the club head to strike the impact bag. You will "feel" all of the qualities of a good swing.

Because there is no ball you will swing freely, as you are not concerned with the result of the swing. This drill will also strengthen your arms and wrists and will create a swing of greater freedom. It will also encourage you to transfer your weight to your front foot on the downswing. If you can carry

The impact bag encourages you to swing freely and also strengthens the arms and hands.

The Pelz Putting Track is an ideal training device. It will help you with both distance and direction.

If you practice properly with the Medicus it will never hinge.

this feeling to the course you will hit the ball farther and more solidly.

Another good full swing training device is the Medicus. This device is a 5 iron with an actual hinge in the shaft. If you use a pure swinging motion, the force you create through the swing will prevent the hinge from working and the shaft will appear normal. If you snatch the club back quickly with your hands or start the club down too early, the hinge in the shaft will release the shaft and it will appear to be bent at a 90-degree angle.

A simple training device to recover the feel of the swing is a large ball (soccer, basketball, or medicine ball). Stand in a good athletic position and hold the ball waist high with both hands. Then toss it! The action of tossing the ball is very similar to swinging a club. As you toss the ball back and forth, you'll feel your weight transfer to your back foot and then your front foot. Your arms and the center of your body swing together as you follow through.

A good teaching device for putting is the Pelz Putting Track. It helps you see the line of the putt as well as learn what size putting stroke you need for different distances.

The action of throwing a soccer ball underhanded is very close to the movement made in a good golf swing. This is a great drill if you have lost the feel of your swing.

Another device to improve putting is a simple string that you affix slightly above the line of a straight putt. You can use two nails, one directly behind the hole and one directly behind the ball. As you address the ball, which is directly below the string, you can easily see if the putter is lined up squarely.

Now test your putting stroke to see how well you follow the string. This is also a great aid to help you visualize the line.

The putting track and the use of a string to practice putting are invaluable tools to learn to see the line of the putt and increase your confidence.

18

PHYSICAL CONDITIONING

Gary Player was the first professional golfer to appreciate the benefit of improved physical conditioning. Player is currently in his fifth decade of championship-level golf!

Aerobic exercise is recommended for general well-being as well as to improve your golf game. Aerobic training is simply aerobic exercise. The main purpose of aerobic exercise is to improve the cardio-respiratory system and general muscle tone. A great benefit of aerobic exercise is that it reduces psychological stress, another phrase for tournament pressure.

Three important characteristics of exercise must be considered: frequency, duration, and intensity.

Frequency. In order to see improvement you should exercise three to five times per week. Exercising once or twice a week will maintain fitness for the most part, but does not provide enough activity to achieve significant gains in aerobic fitness.

Duration. The duration of the exercise must be at least 15 minutes. The best gains are achieved when the duration is extended to 30 or 60 minutes per session. There is nothing wrong with exercising for over an hour if you are easily able to do it.

Intensity. The intensity of the exercise is more difficult to measure than the frequency or duration, and you may need a professional trainer to help measure the intensity. Generally, the exercise should be intense enough so that your heart rate increases.

Weight training. The two basic types of weight training are free weights and training equipment machines. Each program will vary depending upon the golfer's needs but in general it should include a lot of repetitions with fairly light weights or resistance rather than heavy weights with fewer repetitions. Golfers are not trying to build bulky muscles but long, supple ones. The goal is to increase strength without loosing flexibility.

Hand strength. An overlooked factor in achieving distance with a given golf club is hand strength. You create power through your swing. That power is most efficiently transmitted if your hands are strong. This does not mean that you should hold onto the handle of the club tightly. Grip pressure should always be medium-soft. But there is a direct correlation between hand strength and distance. A simple way to increase hand strength is to exercise with a rubber ball or a hand exerciser made from a putty-type material. Exercise your weaker hand (if there is a big difference in strength between your two hands), so that eventually they are close to equal. In a short period of time you will increase your hand strength by at least ten percent. Doing this will add a few yards to your tee shot.

► SOME FINAL THOUGHTS

Golfers all want to be consistent in their ability to hit the ball solidly. The key to consistency is balance. All physical activity that appears graceful is a result of good balance.

Keep it simple. You can easily become very confused about your golf swing. A quick-fix gimmick will often create another problem in your swing that will lead to another compensation, and so on and so on. Stick to the proven fundamentals—they always work.

Find a good teacher. The PGA and LPGA set high standards for teachers. Find one whom you are comfortable with both as a person and teacher. You may not have to visit the teacher often, maybe only a few times a year for a "check-up." Don't wait for your game to fall apart before you look for professional help. That makes it harder for both you and the teacher. It's a good idea to take a lesson when you're playing well. That's the perfect time to take the quality of your game to the next level.

Play at a good pace. Always be ready to hit when it's your turn. Line up your next shot as your playing partners are lining up theirs. Playing a fairly quick pace makes the game more enjoyable for all. Remember, very slow players are not often asked to join the foursome.

When you are playing, try to visualize your next shot and do not worry about swing mechanics. Save swing changes for the practice tee.

Golf is a sport. It requires rhythm and balance as every sport does.

Good luck! I hope you continue to enjoy this wonderful game for a lifetime!

DIRECTORY OF GOLF TERMS

Ace: A hole scored in one stroke.

Addressing the ball: A player has addressed the ball when he has taken his stance by placing his feet in position for and in preparation of making a stroke and has also grounded his club. In a hazard a player has addressed the ball when he has taken his stance in preparation of making a stroke.

All square: An even score, neither side being a hole up.

Approach: A stroke or shot to the putting green.

Apron: The last few yards of fairway in front of the green.

Away: The farthest from the hole.

Backspin: Backward rotation of the ball, causing it to stop abruptly.

Bent grass: A species of grass used for putting greens.

Best ball: Match in which a single player competes against the best ball of two or more.

Birdie: One stroke under par for a hole.

Blind: An approach position from which the green cannot be seen.

Bogey: One stroke over par for a hole.

Borrow or break: In putting, to play to either side of the direct line from the ball to the hole to compensate for roll or slant in the green.

Bunker: An area of bare ground, often a marked depression, usually covered with sand.

Bye holes: Holes remaining after a match is finished, that is, after one side is more holes up than remain for play.

Caddie: A person who carries a player's clubs.

Carry: Distance from where a ball is hit to where it first strikes the ground.

Casual water: Any temporary accumulation of water, such as a puddle after rain.

Chip: Short approach shot, on which the ball flies close to the ground.

Concede: To grant that an opponent has won a hole before play has been completed.

Course: The terrain over which the game is played; the whole area within which play is permitted.

Cup: The hole into which the ball is played, $4^1/4$ inches in diameter and at least 4 inches deep.

Default: To concede a match to an opponent without playing against him; to fail to appear for a scheduled match.

Divot: A piece of grass cut out by a club during a stroke. Divots should always be replaced before the player moves on.

Dog-leg: A hole that bends sharply to left or right between tee and green.

Down: In match play, a side is down when it has lost more holes than it has won.

Draw: Controlled hook.

Dub: An unskillful player; also, to hit the ball poorly.

Eagle: Two strokes under par for a hole.

Face: Slope of a bunker; part of the club head that strikes the ball.

Fade: Controlled slice.

Fairway: The closely cut turf intended for play between tee and green.

Flagstick: Movable straight indicator, usually a lightweight pole with a numbered flag, placed in the hole to show its location; sometimes referred to as the pin.

Follow-through: Continuation of the swing of the club after the ball has been struck.

"Fore!": Warning cry by a player to any person in the way of his ball.

Forecaddie: A person employed to indicate the position of balls on the course.

Four-ball match: A match in which there are two players to a side, each side playing its better ball against the better ball of the other side.

Foursome: A match in which there are two players to a side, each side playing one ball.

Green: Putting green around a hole.

Gross: A player's score before deducting any handicap.

Ground: To sole or rest the club lightly on the ground, in preparing to strike the ball.

Ground under repair: Any portion of the course under repair or maintenance. If a ball should land on ground under repair or if the ground under repair should interfere with the players stance or swing, the ball may be lifted and dropped, without penalty, as near as possible to where it lay, but not nearer the hole.

Halved: A hole is halved when each side has taken the same number of strokes.

Handicap: The number of strokes a player receives to adjust his score to a common level, the generally accepted common level being scratch, or zero-handicap golf.

Hanging: A hanging ball is one which lies on a downslope.

Hazard: Any bunker or water hazard.

Heel: Part of the club head nearest the shaft; to hit from this part and send the ball at right angles to the line of play.

Hole: The hole into which the ball is played (see CUP); one of the 18 units, or holes, on a course, consisting of teeing ground, fairway, rough, hazards, and putting green.

Hole-high: A ball that lies even with the hole (cup) but to one side or the other.

Hole out: Make the final stroke in playing the ball into the hole.

Honor: The privilege of driving off, or playing from the teeing ground first.

Hook: To curve the ball widely to the left.

Hosel: Socket on the club head into which the shaft is fitted.

Lateral water hazard: A water hazard running approximately parallel to the line of play and so situated that it is impractical to keep the spot at which a ball crosses the hazard margin between the player and the hole.

Lie: The inclination of a club when held on the ground in the natural position for striking; the situation of the ball.

Line: The direction in which a player desires his ball to travel.

Links: A golf course, especially a seaside course.

Loft: To elevate the ball; backward slant of the face of the club.

Long game: The strokes where attaining distance is the more important factor.

Loose impediments: Natural object not fixed or growing, as a stone, leaf or twig.

Marker: A scorer in stroke play appointed by a tournament committee to record a competitor's score; a marker indicating the front edge of a teeing ground or the boundaries of a hole.

Match play: Reckoning the score by holes won and lost.

Medal play: Stroke play.

Mixed foursome: Foursome in which a man and a woman play as partners.

Nassau: A system or scoring under which one point is awarded for winning the first 9 holes, one for the second 9, and a third for the full 18.

Net: Score after deducting handicap.

Observer: Person appointed by a tournament committee to assist a referee in deciding questions of fact and to report to him any breach of a rule or local rule.

Obstruction: Anything artificial that has been erected, placed, or left on the course.

Out of bounds: Ground on which play is prohibited.

Outside agency: Referee, observer, marker, forecaddie, or other outside agency not a part of the match or, in stroke play, not a part of a player's side.

Par: Theoretically perfect play, or the score an expert would be expected to make on a hole, calculated on the number of strokes required to reach the green plus two putts. Par is calculated on the basis of distance. Women's par for a course is slightly higher than par for men. USGA standards for computing par are:

	Men's Par	Women's Par
Par 3	up to 250 yd.	up to 210 yd.
Par 4	251 to 470 yd.	211 to 400 yd.
Par 5	471 and over	401 to 575 yd.
Par 6		576 yd. and over

Penalty stroke: A stroke added to the score of a side under certain rules.

Pin: A rod or pole to which a flag is attached (see Flagstick).

Pitch: An approach on which the ball is lofted in a high arc (see CHIP).

Pitch and run: An approach on which a part of the desired distance is covered by the roll of the ball after it strikes the ground.

Pivot: The turn of the body as a stroke is played.

Pull: To hit the ball so that it will curve to the left.

Putt: Stroke made on a putting green.

Putting green: All ground of the hole being played that is specially prepared for putting or is otherwise defined as such by the committee.

Referee: Person appointed by the tournament committee to accompany players to decide questions of fact and rules of golf.

Rough: Long grass bordering the fairway, also at times between tee and fairway; may include bushes, trees, etc.

Rub of the green: Any deflection or stoppage of a ball by an outside agency; the ball is played as it lies, without penalty.

Run: To run a ball along the ground in an approach instead of chipping or pitching it; distance a ball rolls after it lands.

Sand trap: A bunker having a layer of sand (see BUNKER).

Scratch player: One who receives no handicap allowance.

Short game: Approach shots and putts.

Single: Match between two players.

Slice: To curve the ball widely to the right.

Square: When a match is even.

Stance: The position of a player's feet and body when addressing the ball.

Stroke: Forward movement of the club with the intention of fairly striking the ball.

Stroke hole: Hole on which a handicap stroke is given.

Tee: An artificial peg or a pinch of sand on which the ball may be placed for the first stroke on each hole.

Teeing ground: Starting place for the hole to be played, indicated by two marks on the ground; also called the tee.

Three ball match: Match in which three play against one another, each playing his own ball.

Threesome: Match in which one player competes against two, who play alternate strokes with the same ball.

Through the green: The whole area of the course except hazards and the teeing ground and putting green of the hole being played.

Up: In match play, a side is up when it has won more holes than it has lost.

Water hazard: Any water (except casual water) or water course, regardless of whether is contains water.

▶ INDEX